Presented to _____

On this _____ day of_____

by _____

With this special message:

_____

_____

_____

The Glory of Spring

THOMAS NELSON PUBLISHERS
Nashville, Tennessee

Copyright © 1994 by Thomas Nelson Publishers

Published in Nashville, Tennessee by Thomas Nelson Publishers.

**Library of Congress
Cataloging-in-Publication Data**

Glory of spring.
      p.   cm. — (Itty Bitty books)
  ISBN 0-8407-6341-7 (TR)
  ISBN 0-7852-8339-0 (MM)
   1. Spring—Quotations, maxims, etc.
  2. Spring—Poetry. I. Series: Itty Bitty book.
PN6084.S73G56 1994
808.81′933—dc20   93-21543 CIP

Printed in Singapore.
1 2 3 4 5 —98 97 96 95 94

INTRODUCTION

This little book was created just for you. It is a celebration of Spring—that most glorious season of the year that harbors hope, renews faith and fulfills a human longing to believe in the beautiful. Spring is as special as you are to me. May you be blessed with many more springtimes in your life.

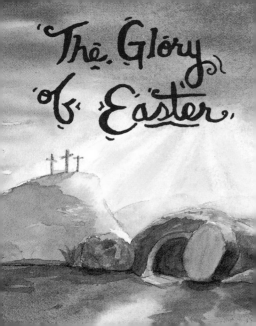

Now on the first day of the week, very early in the morning, they, and certain other women with them, came to the tomb bringing the spices which they had prepared. But they found the stone rolled away from the tomb. And it happened, as they were greatly perplexed about this, that behold, two men stood by them in shining garments.

Then, as they were afraid
and bowed their faces to the
earth, they said to them,
"Why do you seek the living
among the dead? He is not
here, but is risen!"

—*Luke 24:1-7*

I am the good shepherd; and I know My sheep, and am known by My own. As the Father knows Me, even so I know the Father; and I lay down My life for the sheep.

—*John 10:14–15*

Our LORD has written the promise of resurrection, not in books alone, but in every leaf of springtime.

—*Martin Luther*

There's sacredness in God's
  great plan
And his last Gethsemane.
For victory rode his darkest
  hour
With hope for you and me.
  —*Mamie Ozburn Odum*

Nature is the art of God.

—Dante

Easter is the New Year's Day of the soul.

—A. B. Simpson

The garden's alive with
Easter.
O, may your heart's garden
be, too,
That your life might bloom
with beauty,
Revealing Christ's love in
you.

—*Loise Pinkerton Fritz*

We wait for thy coming,
  sweet wind of the south,
For the touch of thy light
  wings, the kiss of thy
  mouth,
For the yearly evangel thou
  bearest from God,
Resurrection and life to the
  graves of the sod!

—John Greenleaf Whittier

There is a miracle in every
new beginning.

—*Herman Hesse*

Slayer of Winter, art thou
  here again?
O welcome, thou that
  bring'st the Summer nigh!
  —*William Morris*

The nicest thing about the
promise of Spring is that
sooner or later she'll have
to keep it.
  —*Mark Beltaire*

A lily of a day
Is fairer in May,
Although it fall and die that
    night;
It was a plant and flower of
    light.
In small proportions we just
    beauties see;
And in short measures, life
    may perfect be.

—Ben Jonson

My beloved spoke, and said
   to me:
"Rise up, my love, my fair
   one,
And come away.
For lo, the Winter is past,
The rain is over and gone.
The flowers appear on the
   earth;
The time of singing has
   come,
And the voice of the
   turtledove
Is heard in our land."

—*Song of Solomon 2:10–12*

Autumn arrives in the early morning, but Spring at the close of a Winter day.

—Elizabeth Bowen

The year's at the Spring
And day's at the morn;
Morning's at seven;
The hillside's dew-pearled;
The lark's on the wing;
The snail's on his thorn;
God's in His heaven—
All's right with the world.

—Robert Browning

Hard is the heart that loved
naught in May.

—*Geoffery Chaucer*

Sweet Spring, full of sweet
days and roses,
A box where sweets
compacted lie.

—*George Herbert*

The country habit has me by
   the heart,
For he's bewitched for ever
   who has seen,
Not with his eyes but with
   his vision,
Spring
Flow down the woods and
   stipple leaves with sun.
               —*Vita Sackville-West*

Spring has returned. The earth is like a child that knows poems.

—*Rainer Maria Rilke*

———

When the hounds of Spring
   are on Winter's traces,
The mother of months in
   meadow or plain
Fills the shadows and windy
   places
With lisp of leaves and ripple
   of rain.

—*Algernon Charles
   Swinburne*

Spring is coming home with
her world-wandering feet.
And all things are made
young with young desires.

—*Francis Thompson*

———

When Spring is dancing
among the hills, one should
not stay in a little dark
corner.

—*Kahlil Gibran*

When, loosened from the
   Winter's bond,
The Spring appears,
The birds that were silent
Come out and sing,
The flowers that were
   prisoned
Come out and bloom.

—*Nukada*

A little Madness in the Spring
Is wholesome even for the
  king,
But God be with the Clown.
  —Emily Dickinson

———

Never yet was a springtime
  When the buds forgot to
  blow.
  —Margaret Sangster

I know there will be Spring;
as surely as the birds know
it when they see above the
snow two tiny, quivering
green leaves. Spring cannot
fail us.

—*Olive Schreiner*

I thought that Spring must
last forevermore,
For I was young and loved,
and it was May.

—*Vera Brittain*

I love the morning more than
the evening, the Spring more
than the Fall. The promise
more than the fulfillment.

—*Raisa Orlova*

A trap's a very useful thing:
Nature in our path sets
Spring.
—*Mary Carolyn Davies*

————

No one thinks of Winter
when the grass is green!
—*Rudyard Kipling*

If Winter comes, can Spring be far behind?

—*Percy Bysshe Shelley*

No Winter lasts forever, no Spring skips its turn. April is a promise that May is bound to keep and we know it.

—*Hal Borland*

Spring never is Spring unless
it comes too soon.

—*G. K. Chesterton*

Wag the world how it will,
Leaves must be green in
Spring.

—*Herman Melville*

The world's favorite season is the Spring. All things seem possible in May.

—*Edwin Way Teale*

In the Spring a young man's fancy lightly turns to thoughts of love.

—*Alfred, Lord Tennyson*

A hush is over everything—
Silent as women wait for
  love,
The world is waiting for the
  Spring.

—*Sara Teasdale*

Come, gentle Spring!
ethereal Mildness! come.

—*James Thomson*

———

April, April,
Laugh thy girlish laughter;
Then, the moment after,
Weep thy girlish tears!

—*Sir William Watson*

March is a tomboy with tousled hair, a mischievous smile, mud on her shoes and a laugh in her voice

—*Hal Borland*

———

Into every empty corner, into all forgotten things and nooks, Nature struggles to pour life, pouring life into the dead, life into life itself.

—*Henry Beston*

Man is wise and constantly
in quest of more wisdom;
but the ultimate wisdom,
which deals with
beginnings, remains
locked in a seed.

—Hal Borland

One touch of Nature makes
the whole world kin.
—**William Shakespeare**

———

God almighty first planted a
garden.
—*Francis Bacon*

How cunningly nature hides
every wrinkle of her
inconceivable antiquity
under roses and violets
and morning dew!
—Ralph Waldo Emerson

The kiss of the sun for
  pardon,
The song of the birds for
  mirth.
One is nearer God's heart in
  a garden
Than anywhere else on
  earth.

—Dorothy Gurney

Each flower is a soul
opening out to nature.
        —*Gerard de Nerval*

There is material enough in a
single flower for the
ornament of a score of
cathedrals.
                —*John Ruskin*

I wandered lonely as a cloud
That floats on high o'er vales
  and hills,
When all at once I saw a
  crowd,
A host of golden daffodils.
—*William Wordsworth*

You fight dandelions all weekend, and late Monday afternoon there they are, pert as all get out, in full and gorgeous bloom, pretty as can be, thriving as only dandelions can in the face of adversity.

—*Hal Borland*

A weed is no more than a
    flower in disguise,
Which is seen through at
    once, if love give a man
    eyes.
        —James Russell Lowell

In springtime, the only pretty
    ring time,
When birds do sing, hey ding
    a ding, ding:
Sweet lovers love the Spring.
    —*William Shakespeare*

When daffodils begin to
   peer,
With heigh! the doxy over
   the dale,
Why, then comes in the
   sweet o' the year;
For the red blood reigns in
   the Winter's pale.

        —William Shakespeare

In those vernal seasons of the year, when the air is calm and pleasant, it were an injury and sullenness against Nature not to go out and see her riches and partake in her rejoicing with heaven and earth.

—*John Milton*

Spring hangs her infant
blossom on the trees,
Rock'd in the cradle of
western breeze.
—*William Cowper*

———

And 'tis my faith that every
flower
Enjoys the air it breathes.
—*William Wordsworth*

In days when daisies deck
   the ground,
And blackbirds whistle clear,
With honest joy our hearts
   will bound
To see the coming year.

—Robert Burns

Now fades the last long
   streak of snow,
Now burgeons every maze
   of quick
About the flowering squares,
   and think
By ashen roots the violets
   blow.

   —*Alfred, Lord Tennyson*

When daisies pied and
    violets blue
And lady-smocks all
    silver-white
And cuckoo-buds of yellow
    hue
Do paint the meadows with
    delight.

—William Shakespeare

Here the cool mosses deep,
And thro' the moss the ivies
  creep,
And in the stream the
  long-leaved flowers weep,
And from the craggy ledge
  the poppy hangs in sleep.
      —*Alfred, Lord Tennyson*

When the green woods
   laugh, with the voice of joy
And the dimpling stream
   runs laughing by,
When the air does laugh with
   our merry wit,
And the green hill laughs
   with the noise of it.

            —*William Blake*

I sing of brooks, of
   blossoms, bird, and
   bowers:
Of April, May, of June, and
   July flowers.
I sing of Maypoles,
   Hock-carts, wassails,
   wakes,
Of bridegrooms, brides, and
   of their bridal cakes.
                    —Robert Herrick

Is it so small a thing
To have enjoyed the sun,
To have lived light in the
    Spring?

—*Matthew Arnold*

———

Winter lingered so long in
the lap of Spring that it
occasioned a great deal
of talk.

—*Bill Nye*

For Winter's rains and ruins
  are over,
And all the season of snows
  and sins. . . .
And frosts are slain and
  flowers begotten,
And in green underwood
  and cover
Blossom by blossom the
  Spring begins.

—*Algernon Charles
  Swinburne*

Four ducks on a pond,
A grass bank beyond,
A blue sky of Spring,
White clouds on the wing;
What a little thing
To remember for years—

—William Allingham

They spoke, I think, of perils
   past.
They spoke, I think, of peace
   at last.
One thing I remember;
Spring came on forever,
Spring came on forever.

—*Vachel Lindsay*

That God once loved a
   garden
We learn in Holy writ.
And seeing gardens in the
   Spring
I well can credit it.

—Winifred Mary Letts

If God took time to create beauty, how can we be too busy to appreciate it?

—*Randall B. Corbin*

Like life, few gardens have only flowers.

—*Anonymous*

———

Now Spring restores balmy warmth.

—*Catullus*

Like a lovely woman late for
  her appointment
She's suddenly here, taking
  us unawares,
So beautifully annihilating
  expectation
That we applaud her
  punctual arrival.

—Gerald Bullett

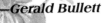

What is a weed? A plant
    whose virtues have not
yet been discovered.
—Ralph Waldo Emerson

———

Soft maids and village hinds
    shall bring
Each opening sweet of
    earliest bloom,
And rifle all the breathing
    Spring.
—William Collins

Sweet Auburn, loveliest
village of the plain,
Where health and plenty
cheered the labouring
swain,
Where smiling Spring its
earliest visit paid,
And parting Summer's
lingering blooms delayed.
—*Oliver Goldsmith*

Alas, that Spring should
   vanish with the Rose!
That Youth's sweet-scented
   Manuscript should close!
The Nightingale that in the
   Branches sang,
Ah, whence, and whither
   flown again, who knows!

—*Edward Fitzgerald*

This was one of my prayers: for a parcel of land not so very large, which should have a garden and a spring of ever-flowing water near the house, and a bit of woodland as well as these.

—Horace

Spring, the sweet Spring, is
  the year's pleasant king;
Then blooms each thing,
  then maids dance in a ring,
Cold doth not sting, the
  pretty birds do sing:
Cuckoo, jug-jug, pu-we,
  to-witta-woo.

—Ogden Nash

Gone were but the Winter,
Come were but the Spring,
I would go to a covert
Where the birds sing.

—*Christina Rossetti*

———

The merry cuckoo,
   messenger of Spring,
His trumpet shrill hath thrice
   already sounded.

—*Edmund Spenser*

I dreamed that, as I
wandered by the way,
Bare Winter suddenly was
changed to Spring,
And gentle odors led my
steps astray,
Mixed with a sound of
water's murmuring
Along a shelving bank of
turf, which lay
Under a copse, and hardly
dared to fling
Its green arms round the
bosom of the stream,
But kissed it and then fled,
as thou mightst in dream.

—Percy Bysshe Shelley

Who are the violets now
That strew the green lap of
the new come Spring?

—*William Shakespeare*

Each day is God's gift to you.
Make it blossom and grow
into a thing of beauty.

—*Anonymous*

Fresh Spring the herald of
  love's mighty king,
In whose coat armor richly
  are displayed
All sorts of flowers the which
  on earth do Spring
In goodly colors gloriously
  arrayed.

—Edmund Spenser

A touch divine—
And the scaled eyeball owns
the mystic rod;
Visibly through His garden
walketh God.

—Robert Browning

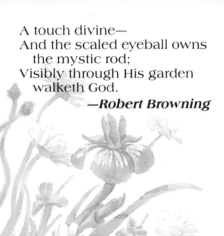

I have a garden of my own,
But so with roses overgrown,
And lilies, that you would it
   guess
To be a little wilderness.
                —*Andrew Marvell*

But all the gardens
Of Spring and Summer were
blooming in the tall tales
Beyond the border and
under the lark full cloud.

—Dylan Thomas

Rose plot,
Fringed pool,
Ferned grot—
The veriest school
Of Peace.

—Thomas Brown

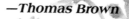

I know a little garden close
Set thick with lily and red
   rose,
Where I would wander if I
   might
From dewy dawn to dewy
   night.

—William Morris

All my life through, the new sights of Nature made me rejoice like a child.

—*Marie Curie*

———

To me the meanest flower
   that blows can give
Thoughts that do often lie
   too deep for tears.

—*William Wordsworth*

The Dandelion's pallid tube
Astonishes the Grass,
And Winter instantly becomes
An infinite Alas—

—Emily Dickinson

That of all the flowers in the
   field,
Then love I most these
   flowers white and red,
Such as men call daisies in
   our town.

—*Geoffrey Chaucer*

All nature wears one universal grin.

—Henry Fielding

Earth fills her lap with pleasures of her own.

—William Wordsworth

When in April the sweet
    showers fall
And pierce the drought of
    March to the root, and all
The veins are bathed in
    liquor of such power
As brings about the
    engendering of the flower.

—Geoffrey Chaucer

May never was the month of
  love,
For May is full of flowers;
But rather April, wet by kind,
For love is full of showers.
—Robert Southwell

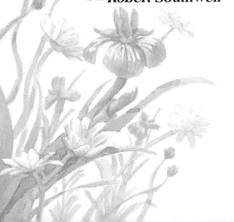

To see a world in a grain of
sand
And a heaven in a wild
flower,
Hold infinity in the palm of
your hand
And eternity in an hour.

—*William Blake*

The Tale of Peter Rabbit

Once upon a time there were four little Rabbits, and their names were—Flopsy, Mopsy, Cotton-tail, and Peter. "Now, my dears," said old Mrs. Rabbit one morning, "you may go into the fields or down the lane, but don't go into Mr. McGregor's garden."

Flopsy, Mopsy, and Cotton-tail, who were good little bunnies, went down the lane to gather blackberries; but Peter, who was very naughty, ran straight away to Mr.

McGregor's garden, and squeezed under the gate! First he ate some lettuces and some French beans; and then he ate some radishes; and then, feeling rather sick, he went to look for some parsley.

But 'round the end of a cucumber frame, whom should he meet but Mr. McGregor, who jumped up and ran after Peter, waving a rake and calling out, "Stop thief!"

Peter was most dreadfully

frightened; he rushed all over the garden, for he had forgotten the way back to the gate. I think he might have gotten away altogether if he had not unfortunately run into a gooseberry net, and got caught by the large buttons on his jacket.

Mr. McGregor came up with a sieve, which he intended to pop upon the top of Peter. Peter wriggled out just in time, leaving his jacket behind him, rushed into the tool-shed, and jumped into a can. It would have been a beautiful thing to hide in, if it had not had so much water in it. Presently, Peter sneezed, "Kertyschoo!" Mr. McGregor tried to put his foot upon Peter, who jumped out of a window and started running as fast as he could go. He slipped underneath the gate, and was safe at last in the wood outside the garden.

Mr. McGregor hung up the little jacket for a scarecrow to frighten the blackbirds.

I am sorry to say that Peter was not very well during the evening. His mother put him to bed, and made some camomile tea; and she gave a dose of it to Peter! But Flopsy, Mopsy, and Cotton-tail had bread and milk and blackberries for supper.

—Beatrix Potter

The End